CONSTITUTION

AND

DISCIPLINE

OF THE

METHODIST CHURCH.

———::::———

SPRINGFIELD, OHIO:
A. H. BASSETT, PUBLISHING AGENT.
1867

HISTORICAL PREFACE.

THE METHODIST CHURCH, whose government, faith and practice are here given, like original Methodism, is a child of Providence. Those who compose it were urged to its organization by considerations as sacred as those which bound them to Christ. In vindication of their motives, they need only recite a few plain facts.

A large portion now constituting this church were formerly Methodist Protestants. These were such in opposition to Episcopacy, and an exclusively ministerial government, as characterizing the elder and more numerous branch of the Methodist family. Their origin dates back to 1820—1830. During these years of earnest discussion it was made apparent that the M. E. ministry would relinquish nothing of the power they had hitherto assumed and withheld from the people. Indeed, in 1828 their General Conference declared, as its settled faith, that 'the great Head of the Church had imposed on them the duty of preaching the gospel, of administering its ordinances, and of *maintaining its moral discipline among those over whom the Holy Ghost had made them overseers!'* It also claimed that the "divinely instituted ministry" had resting upon them the duty of not permitting the administration of discipline to pass from their hands. Those, like A. Shinn, N. Snethen and others, who were opposed to Episcopacy and an exclusively ministerial government, had but one alternative left, viz: the organization of a new body. This they accepted. Hence the origin of the Methodist Protestant Church.

The other principal element in the Methodist Church are those formerly known as Wesleyan Methodists. This body originated as the result of the Anti-Slavery struggle in the M. E. Church. It was not merely that Slavery was in that church, but because that church endorsed it and threw its shield over it. Those who sought the removal of Slavery therefrom, found that Episcopal prerogative and church action stood between them and the evil they would destroy. To leave was their only relief. Had the M. E. Church allowed O. Scott and others the same liberty against Slavery they did against other sins, Slavery alone would not have driven them out. Episcopacy and church sanctioning of sin were the real causes of the origin of Wesleyan Methodism. Had the Methodist Protestants at this time been free from connection with Slavery, the Wesleyans would have gone into it. In governmental views they were substantially agreed. But the M. P. Church, like the M. E. Church, was involved in Slavery, and about half its strength lay within the slave-holding States.

The Conferences lying within the Free States finally became convinced that they could not persuade their Southern brethren to abandon Slavery, and suspended co-operation with them. Nineteen Annual Conferences united in a call for a General Convention, which assembled at Springfield, Ohio, Nov. 10, 1858.

This Convention declared that in its judgment, "the practice of buying and selling men, women and children, or holding them in slavery, as they are held in these United

States, is inconsistent with the morality of the Holy Scriptures; and did further declare all official connection, co-operation and official fellowship with such Conferences and Churches within the Methodist Protestant Association as practice or tolerate slave-holding or slave-trading, to be suspended until the evil complained of be removed."

The Convention further, in obedience to instructions from its constituents, ordered the removal from the Constitution and Discipline of such words and clauses as make distinction on account of color, and such as had been understood to protect ministers and members of the church in the practice of slave-holding and slave-trading.

In 1862, another General Convention was held in Cincinnati, which adopted a preamble and resolutions, in which they affirmed in substance,

1. That the Methodist Protestant Church was firmly bound to be loyal to the Government of the United States, as set forth in the 23d Article of Religion.

2. That the States of South Carolina, North Carolina, Georgia, Alabama, Mississippi, Florida, Louisiana, Texas, Tennessee, Arkansas, and the eastern part of Virginia, including

the Methodist Protestant Church in those States, had renounced their allegiance to the United States, and were then in armed rebellion against the Government of our country.

3. That the position assumed by the Methodist Protestant Church in the rebel States aforenamed, in repudiating the 23d Article of Religion, and taking part in the rebellion, must be considered in the light of a revolt from the Methodist Protestant Church.

The above action on the part of the Methodist Protestant Church, removed the only essential difference between them and the Wesleyan Methodist Connection, and opened the way for the union of the two bodies.

A preliminary Convention was held in Cleveland, Ohio, in June, 1865, in which a number of independent Churches were represented, and resulted in a unanimous agreement upon general principles of Union, and in a call for another Convention, which assembled at Cincinnati, May 9, 1866. This Convention agreed upon a basis of union between the Methodist Protestant Church and the Wesleyan Methodist Connection, and such independent Non-Episcopal Churches as were represented therein, or as might choose to come into the Union. The Convention adopted Elementary Principles and a Constitution, and provided for the preparation of a Discipline, all of which are hereinafter contained.

The First General Conference provided for by the Cincinnati Convention, had for its work the revision and adoption of the Discipline which follows. This it did, and as we think with scrupulous fidelity to the Constitution adopted at Cincinnati. It is commended for its simplicity, its recognition of the rights of the laity, and as providing for efficient church action. The undersigned, as a committee to edit the action of the Conference, have thought it proper to introduce their work with these explanatory statements. In so doing they have but done what all compilers, even of State and National Statutes, are accustomed to do. For their action in this matter they ask but the usual courtesy extended to such as perform like duties.

GEO. BROWN,
JNO. SCOTT,
A. H. BASSETT,
H. B. KNIGHT.
Editing Committee.

CONSTITUTION

OF THE

METHODIST CHURCH

PREAMBLE.

WE, the Representatives of the Methodist Churches, in General Convention assembled, acknowledging the Lord Jesus Christ as the only head of the Church, and the Word of God as the sufficient rule of faith and practice, in all things pertaining to godliness; and being fully persuaded that the representative form of Church government is the most scriptural, best suited to our condition, and most congenial with our views and feelings as fellow-citizens with the saints, and of the household of God; and, Whereas, a written Constitution, establishing the form of government, and securing to the Ministers and Members of the Church their rights and privileges, is the best safeguard of Christian liberty; We, therefore, trusting in the protection of Almighty God, and acting in the name and by the authority of our constituents, do ordain and establish, and agree to be governed by the following elementary principles and Constitution:

ELEMENTARY PRINCIPLES.

1. A Christian Church is a society of believers in Jesus Christ, assembling in any one place for religious worship, and is of Divine institution.

2. Christ is the Head of the Church, and the Word of God the only rule of faith and conduct.

3. No person who loves the Lord Jesus Christ, and obeys the Gospel of God our Savior, ought to be deprived of Church membership.

4. Every man has an inalienable right to private judgment in matters of religion, and an equal right to express his opinion, in any way which will not violate the laws of God or the rights of his fellowmen.

5. Church trials should be conducted on

Gospel principles only; and no minister or member should be excommunicated, except for immorality, the propagation of unchristian doctrines, or for neglect of duties enjoined by the Word of God.

6. The Pastoral or Ministerial office and duties are of Divine appointment; and all Elders in the Church of God are equal; but ministers are forbidden to be lords over God's heritage, or to have dominion over the faith of the saints.

7. The Church has a right to form and enforce such rules and regulations only, as are in accordance with the Holy Scriptures, and may be necessary, or have a tendency to carry into effect the great system of practical Christianity. The Church ought to secure to all her official bodies the necessary authority for the purposes of good government.

8. Whatever power may be necessary to the formation of rules and regulations, is inherent in the ministers and members of the churches; but so much of that power may be delegated, from time to time, upon a plan of representation, as they may judge necessary and proper; provided, that they create no distinct and independent sovereignties.

9. It is the duty of all ministers and

members of the Church to maintain godliness, and to oppose all moral evil.

10. It is obligatory on ministers of the gospel to be faithful in the discharge of their pastoral and ministerial duties; and it is also obligatory on members to esteem ministers highly for their work's sake, and to render them a righteous compensation for their labors.

CONSTITUTION.

Article I.

The name of this religious body shall be THE METHODIST CHURCH.

Article II.—Terms of Membership.

SEC. 1. The conditions required of those who apply for probationary membership in a church are, a desire to flee from the wrath to come, and be saved by grace through faith in our Lord Jesus Christ, with an avowed determination to walk in all the commandments of God blameless.

SEC. 2. The churches shall have power to receive members, on profession of faith or on certificate of good standing in any other Christian Church; provided they are satisfied with the Christian experience of the candidates.

Article III.—Reception of Churches.

SEC. 1. Any church agreeing to conform to our Constitution, Book of Discipline, and Means of Grace, may, on application to the President of an Annual Conference, to the Pastor of a Church, or to a Quarterly Conference, be received as a member of this body.

SEC. 2. Each church shall have the right to hold and control its own property and manage its own local affairs, independent of all associated relations or bodies.

SEC. 3. It is expected of all churches, as a condition of remaining connected with the general body, that they continue to conform to this Constitution, and the essential regulations contained in the Book of Discipline.

Article IV.—Division of Territory.

SEC. 1. The territory embraced by this Religious Body shall be divided into Districts of convenient size and form; such division to be subject to any changes which the General Conference may from time to time deem necessary.

SEC. 2. Each District shall be divided into Circuits, Stations, and Missions.

Article V.—Quarterly Conferences.

SEC. 1. There shall be a quarterly conference in each pastoral charge, composed of all the ministers, preachers, exhorters, stewards, leaders, trustees, and superintendents of Sabbath-schools, who are members of the church, belonging to the charge, who shall hold four sessions each year; provided that the pastor or a quorum of the quarterly Conference, shall have authority to call special meetings when deemed necessary.

SEC. 2. Each quarterly conference shall have authority to examine into the official character of all its members, and to admonish or reprove them as occasion may require; to grant to persons properly qualified and recommended by the church of which the applicants are members, license to exhort and to preach, and renew their licenses annually; to admit ministers and preachers coming from any other church; to recommend ministers and preachers to the Annual Conference for pastoral work and for ordination; provided, nevertheless, that no person be licensed to preach until he shall have been first examined and recommended by a committee of five, composed of ministers and laymen chosen by the quarterly conference.

Article VI.—Annual Conferences.

SEC. 1. There shall be held, annually,

within the limits of each district, a Conference, composed of all the ministers laboring under its direction, and of one delegate from each circuit, station and mission, for each of its ministers belonging to the Conference; provided, however, that each circuit, station and mission shall have at least one delegate. Each Annual Conference shall regulate the manner of elections in its own district; provided, however, that the election of delegates to the first Annual Conference under this Constitution, shall be according to such regulations as may be adopted for that purpose by the quarterly confercenes of the respective circuits, stations and missions.

SEC. 2. Each Annual Conference shall have authority to elect a President, annually; to examine into the official conduct of its members; to receive, by vote, such ministers and preachers into the Conference as come properly recommended, and who can be efficiently employed as pastors or missionaries; to elect to orders those who are eligible and competent to the pastoral office; to hear and decide on appeals; to define and regulate the boundaries of circuits and stations; and to exercise a general supervision over the pastors and churches, in the following manner and to the following extent:

All ministers and licentiates, who are laboring under the direction of the Conference, shall be at liberty to enter into engagements to serve any pastoral charge for one year from the next session of the Conference; and it shall be the duty of all ministers and licentiates and churches having entered into such arrangements, to report the same to the Conference at its next session.

SEC. 3. Each Annual Conference shall also have authority to perform any other duties which the General Conference may prescribe; and to make such rules and regulations as the peculiarities of the district may require; provided, however, that no rule or regulation may be made inconsistent with this Constitution; and provided furthermore, that the General Conference shall have power to annul any rule or regulation which that body may deem unconstitutional.

Article VII.—General Conferences.

SEC. 1. There shall be a General Conference of this body, held on the third Wednesday of May, 1867, at Cleveland, Ohio, and on the third Wednesday of May every fourth year thereafter, at such place as shall be determined on by the Conference.

SEC. 2. The General Conference shall consist of an equal number of ministers and laymen. The ratio of representation from each Annual Conference district shall be one minister and one layman for every 1,000 persons in full membership; provided, however, that every Annual Conference district that may not have 1,000 members shall be entitled to two representatives,—one minister and one layman,—until a different ratio shall be fixed by the General Conference.

SEC. 3. The representatives to which each Annual Conference district shall be entitled, shall be elected at the time and place of holding the Annual Conference of said district next preceding the sitting of the General Conference, by joint ballot of ministers and laymen.

SEC. 4. The General Conference shall elect by ballot, a President to preside over its deliberations, and one or more Secretaries, to serve during the sitting of the Conference, who shall keep a faithful record of its proceedings; judge of election returns and qualifications of its own members, and form its own rules of order. A majority of the representatives in attendance shall constitute a quorum.

SEC. 5. The ministers and laymen shall deliberate in one body; but if, upon the final passage of any question, it be required by three members, the ministers and laymen shall vote separately; and the concurrence of a majority of both classes of representatives shall be necessary to constitute a vote of the Conference. A similar regulation shall be observed by the Annual Conferences.

SEC. 6. The General Conference shall have authority to make rules and regulations for managing all the general interests of the body, in accordance with the elementary principles and the provisions of this Constitution.

SEC. 7. To determine the ratio of representation to its own body.

SEC. 8. To define the boundaries of Annual Conference districts; provided, however, that the Annual Conferences of any two or more districts shall have power, by mutual agreement, to alter their respective adjoining boundaries, or to set off a new district; but every alteration made in the boundaries of districts shall be reported to the ensuing General Conference, subject to its action.

SEC. 9. The General Conference shall make no rule in violation of the Law of God, or which shall conflict with any of the Elementary Principles, or of this Constitution; or which shall infringe the liberty of speech or of the press; or constitute any order of ministers higher than Elders, or which shall prevent the maintenance of an itinerant ministry.

Article VIII.

OFFICERS.

Presidents of Annual Conferences.

SEC. 1. The President of each Annual Conference shall be elected by ballot, a majority of votes being necessary to a choice, and shall be amenable to that body for his official conduct.

SEC. 2. It shall be the duty of the President of an Annual Conference to preside in all meetings of that body; and, with the assistance of two or more Elders, to ordain such persons as shall be elected to orders; travel through the district—if it be required by the Conference,—and, in the recess of Conference, with the assistance of two or more Elders, to ordain those persons who shall have been elected to orders, and were not present at Conference; to employ such ministers, preachers, and missionaries as are duly recommended, and to make such changes of preachers as may be necessary; provided the consent of the preachers and their charges be first obtained; and to perform such other duties as may be required by his Annual Conference.

Pastors.

The minister or preacher having charge of a station, circuit, or mission, shall be styled the Pastor, and his assistant the Associate Pastor.

All ministers and preachers under the direction of the Conference shall be amenable to that body, and all others shall be amenable to the Quarterly Conferences to which they severally belong.

Class Leaders.

Class Leaders shall be elected annually by their respective classes, or oftener, if necessary.

Conference Stewards.

The Conference Stewards shall be elected annually by the Annual Conferences, and discharge such duties as may be assigned them by the Discipline.

Station and Circuit Stewards.

The Station, Circuit and Mission Stewards shall be elected annually; in the stations, by the members, including ministers and preachers; and in the circuits and missions by the Quarterly Conferences; but every member present, if eighteen years of age, shall be permitted to vote in the election of Stewards. The number of stewards for each circuit, station or mission, to be not less than three, nor more than seven.

Article IX.—General Judiciary.

SEC. 1. Whenever a majority of all the Annual Conferences shall officially call for a judicial decision on any rule or act of the General Conference, it shall be the duty of each and every Annual Conference to appoint, at its next session, one judicial delegate. The delegates thus chosen shall assemble at the place where the General Conference held its last session, on the second Tuesday in May following their appointment.

SEC. 2. A majority of the delegates shall constitute a quorum; and if two-thirds of all present judge said rule or act of the General Conference unconstitutional, they shall have power to declare the same null and void.

SEC. 3. Every decision of the Judiciary

shall be in writing, and shall be published in the periodicals belonging to this body. After the Judiciary shall have performed the duties assigned them in this Constitution, their power shall cease; and no other Judiciary shall be created until after the session of the succeeding General Conference.

Article X.—Special call of the General Conference.

SEC. 1. Two-thirds of the whole number of the Annual Conferences shall have power to call special meetings of the General Conference.

SEC. 2. When it shall have been ascertained that two-thirds of the Annual Conferences have decided in favor of such call, it shall be the duty of the Presidents, or a majority of them, forthwith to designate the time and place of holding the same, and to give due notice to all stations, circuits and missions.

Article XI.—Provision for Altering the Constitution.

SEC. 1. The General Conference shall have power to annul any part of this Constitution, except the second and twelfth articles, and section nine of article seven, by making such alterations or additions as may be recommended in writing by two-thirds of the whole number of the Annual Conferences next preceding the sitting of the General Conference.

SEC. 2. The second and twelfth articles, and the ninth section of article seven of this Constitution, shall be unalterable, except by a General Convention called for the special purpose by two-thirds of the whole number of the Annual Conferences next preceding the General Conference, which convention, and all other conventions of this church, shall be constituted and elected in the same manner and ratio as prescribed for the General Conference. When a General Convention is called by the Annual Conferences, it shall supercede the assembling of the General Conference for that period, and shall have power to discharge all the duties of that body in addition to the particular object for which the Convention shall have been assembled.

Article XII.—Judiciary Principles.

SEC. 1. All offences condemned by the Word of God as being sufficient to exclude a person from the kingdom of grace and glory, shall subject ministers, preachers, and members to expulsion from the church.

SEC. 2. For preaching or disseminating unscriptural doctrines, affecting the general interests of the Christian system, ministers, preachers, and members shall be liable to admonition, and, if incorrigible, to expulsion.

SEC. 3. No minister or preacher shall be deprived of church privileges or ministerial functions, without an impartial trial before a committee of from three to five ministers or preachers, and the right of appeal, the preachers to the ensuing Quarterly, and the ministers to the ensuing Annual Conference.

SEC. 4. No member shall be deprived of church priviliges without an impartial trial. He shall be tried before a committee of three or more lay members, but shall have the right of appeal to the Church, whose decision shall be final.

DISCIPLINE.

Section I.

Articles of Religion.

I.—Of Faith in the Holy Trinity.

There is but one living and true God, everlasting, of infinite power, wisdom and goodness; the Maker and Preserver of all things, visible and invisible. And in unity of this Godhead, there are three persons of one substance, power and eternity;—the Father, the Son, (the Word), and the Holy Ghost.

II.—Of the Son of God.

The only begotten Son of God was conceived by the Holy Ghost, born of the Virgin Mary, suffered under Pontius Pilate, was crucified, dead, and buried; to be a sacrifice, not only for original guilt, but also for the actual sins of men, and to reconcile us to God.

III.—Of the Resurrection of Christ.

Christ did truly rise again from the dead, taking his body with all things appertaining to the perfection of man's nature, wherewith he ascended into heaven, and there sitteth until he return to judge all men at the last day.

IV.—Of the Holy Ghost.

The Holy Ghost, proceeding from the Father and the Son, is of one substance, majesty, and glory, with the Father and the Son, very and eternal God.

V.—The Sufficiency of the Holy Scriptures for Salvation.

The Holy Scriptures contain all things necessary to salvation; so that whatsoever is not read therein, nor may be proved thereby, is not to be required of any man, that it should be believed as an article of faith, or be thought requisite or necessary to salvation. In the name of the Holy Scriptures, we do understand these canonical books of the Old and New Testaments, of whose authority there is no doubt in the church.

The canonical books of the Old Testament are,—Genesis, Exodus, Leviticus, Numbers, Deuteronomy, Joshua, Judges, Ruth, 1. Samuel, 2. Samuel, 1. Kings, 2. Kings, 1. Chronicles, 2. Chronicles, Ezra, Nehemiah, Esther, Job, Psalms, Proverbs, Ecclesiastes, The Song of Solomon, Isaiah, Jeremiah, Lamentations, Ezekiel, Daniel, Hosea, Joel, Amos, Obadiah, Jonah, Micah, Nahum, Habakuk, Zephaniah, Haggai, Zachariah and Malachi.

The canonical books of the New Testament are,—Matthew, Mark, Luke, John, The Acts, The Epistle to the Romans, 1. Corinthians, 2. Corinthians, Galatians, Ephesians, Phillippians, Collossians, 1. Thessalonians, 2. Thessalonians, 1. Timothy, 2. Timothy, Titus, Philemon, Hebrews, James, 1. Peter, 2. Peter, 1. John, 2. John, 3. John, Jude, Revelation.

VI.—Of the Old Testament.

The Old Testament is not contrary to the New; for both in the Old and New Testament everlasting life is offered to mankind through Christ, who is the only Mediator between God and man. Wherefore, they are not to be heard who feign that the old fathers did look only for transitory promises. Although the law given from God by Moses, as touching ceremonies and rites, doth not bind Christians, nor ought the civil precepts thereof of necessity be received in any commonwealth; yet, notwithstanding, no christian, whatsoever, is free from the obedience of the commandments which are called moral.

VII.—Of Relative Duties.

Those two great commandments which require us to love the Lord our God with all our hearts, and our neighbor as ourselves, contain the sum of the Divine law as it is revealed in the Scriptures, and are the measure and perfect rule of human duty, as well for the ordering and directing of families and nations, and all other social bodies, as for individual acts; by which we are required to acknowledge God as our only Supreme Ruler, and all men as created by him, equal in all natural rights. Wherefore, all men are bound so to order all their individual, social and political acts, as to render to God entire and absolute obedience; and to secure to all men the enjoyment of every natural right, as well as to promote the greatest happiness of each in the possession and exercise of such rights.

VIII.—Of Original, or Birth Sin.

Original sin is the corruption of the nature of every man, that naturally is engendered of the offspring of Adam, whereby man is very far gone from original righteousness, and of his own nature inclined to evil, and that continually.

IX.—Of Free Will.

The condition of man after the fall of Adam is such that he cannot turn and prepare himself by his own natural strength and works, to faith and calling upon God; wherefore we have no power to do good works, pleasant and acceptable to God, without the grace of God, by Christ working in us, that we may have a good will, and working with us when we have that good will.

X.—Of the Justification of Man.

We are accounted righteous before God only for the merit of our Lord and Savior Jesus Christ by faith, and not for our own works or deservings;—Wherefore, that we are justified by faith, is a most wholesome doctrine, and very full of comfort.

XI.—Of Good Works.

Although good works, which are the fruit of faith, and follow after justification cannot put away our sins, and endure the severity of God's judgments; yet are they pleasing and acceptable to God in Christ, and spring out of a true and lively faith, insomuch that by them a lively faith may be as evidently known as a tree is discerned by its fruit.

XII.—Of Sin after Justification.

Not every sin willingly committed after justification is the sin against the Holy Ghost, and unpardonable. Wherefore, repentance is not denied to such as fall into sin after justification; after we have received the Holy Ghost, we may depart from grace given, and fall into sin, and by the grace of God rise again and amend our lives.

XIII.—Of Sanctification.

Sanctification is that renewal of our fallen nature by the Holy Ghost, received through faith in Jesus Christ, whose blood of atonement cleanseth from all sin; whereby we are not only delivered from the guilt of sin, but are washed from its pollution, saved from its power, and are enabled, through grace, to love God with all our hearts, and to walk in his holy commandments blameless.

XIV.—Of the Sacraments.

Sacraments, ordained of Christ, are not only badges, or tokens of christian men's profession, but they are certain signs of grace, and God's good will toward us, by which he doth work invisibly in us, and doth not only quicken, but also strengthen and confirm our faith in him.

There are two sacraments ordained of Christ, our Lord, in the Gospel; that is to say, Baptism and the Supper of the Lord.

XV.—Of Baptism.

Baptism is not only a sign of profession, and mark of difference, whereby christians are distinguished from others that are not baptized, but is also a sign of regeneration or the new birth. The baptism of young children is to be retained in the Church.

XVI.—Of the Lord's Supper.

The Supper of the Lord is not only a

sign of the love that christians ought to have among themselves one to another, but rather is a sacrament of our redemption by Christ's death; insomuch that, to such as rightly, worthily, and with faith receive the same, it is made a medium through which God doth communicate grace to the heart.

XVII.—Of the One Oblation of Christ, Finished upon the Cross.

The offering of Christ, once made, is that perfect redemption and propitiation for all the sins of the whole world, both original and actual; and there is none other satisfaction for sin but that alone. Wherefore, to expect salvation on the ground of our own works, or by suffering the pains our sins deserve, either in the present or future state, is derogatory to Christ's offering for us, and a dangerous deceit.

XVIII.—Of the Rites and Ceremonies of Churches.

It is not necessary that rites and ceremonies should in all places be the same, or exactly alike, for they have always been different, and may be changed according to the diversity of countries, times, and men's manners, so that nothing be ordained against God's word.

Every particular Church may ordain, change, or abolish rites and ceremonies, so that all things may be done to edification.

XIX.—Of the Resurrection of the Dead.

There will be a general resurrection of the dead, both of the just and the unjust, at which time the souls and bodies of men will be re-united to receive together a just retribution for the deeds done in the body in this life.

XX.—Of the General Judgment.

There will be a general judgment at the end of the world, when God will judge all men by Jesus Christ, and receive the righteous into his heavenly kingdom, where thay shall be forever secure and happy; and adjudge the wicked to everlasting punishment, suited to the demerit of their sins.

SECTION II.

General Rules.

We hold that the moral teachings of the Bible require—

1. That we do no harm, but avoid evil of every kind; especially those most generally practised; such as

The taking of the name of God in vain.

The profaning the day of the Lord, by ordinary work, or by buying or selling therein.

Drunkenness, or the manufacturing, buying, selling, or using intoxicating liquors, unless for mechanical, chemical, or medicinal purposes; or in any way intentionally aiding others so to do.

The buying or selling of men, women or children, with an intention to enslave them, or holding them as slaves, or claiming that it is right so to do.

Fighting, quarrelling, brawling, brother going to law with brother; returning evil for evil, or railing for railing; the using of many words in buying or selling.

Uncharitable or unprofitable conversation; particularly speaking evil of magistrates and ministers.

Doing unto others as we would not they should do unto us.

Borrowing without a probability of paying; or taking up goods without a probability of paying for them.

2. That we do good by being in every kind merciful after our power, as we have

opportunity, of every possible sort, and, as far as is possible, to all men:

To their bodies, of the ability which God giveth, by giving food to the hungry, by clothing the naked, by visiting or helping them that are sick or in prison:

To their souls, by instructing, reproving, or exhorting all we have any intercourse with; trampling under foot that erroneous doctrine, that "We are not to do good unless *our hearts be free to it:*"

By doing good especially to them that are of the household of faith, or groaning so to be; employing them preferably to others, buying one of another, helping each other in business, and so much the more because the world will love its own:

By all possible *diligence and frugality,* that the Gospel be not blamed:

By running with patience the race that is set before us, *denying ourselves, and taking up our cross daily*; submitting to bear the reproach of Christ; to be as the filth and offscouring of the world, and looking that men should *"say all manner of evil of us falsely, for the Lord's sake."*

3. By attending on all the ordinances of God: such are,

The public worship of God: the ministry of the word, either read or expounded:

The Supper of the Lord: family and private prayer: searching the Scriptures and meditating thereon.

SECTION III.

Admission to Membership.

[*See Constitution, Article II.*]

1. Application for admission to probationary membership should be made to the Pastor of the church, but in case of his absence, to the Associate Pastor, or to a leader, who shall present the names to the church, and if there be no objection, the names of the applicants shall be entered upon the record as probationers. In case objections are made, the question of admission shall be decided by a majority vote of the church, and they shall be recorded as probationers, and the church may admit them to full membership at such time as it shall be satisfied with their christian experience.

2. Persons who have been baptized may be admitted to full membership, by a majority of the church, on profession of faith,

or on certificate, or other satisfactory evidence of good and regular standing in any other church; provided the church is satisfied with the Christian character and experience of the candidates.

3. In cases where it is practicable, we recommend the use of the following form in the reception of members into full connection. After the vote of reception has been taken, the candidate, or candidates, standing before the church, let the officiating minister read the following covenant to them:

COVENANT.

You do solemnly and severally confess the LORD JEHOVAH, FATHER, SON, and HOLY GHOST, to be your God, the object of your supreme affections and your portion forever. You cordially accept the Lord Jesus Christ to be your Redeemer, and the Holy Spirit your Sanctifier, Comforter and Guide.

You cheerfully devote yourselves to God in the everlasting convenant of His grace, consecrating all your powers and faculties to His service and glory. And you promise that you will cleave to Him as your chief good; that you will give diligent attention to HIS word and ordinances; that you will seek the honor and advancement of His kingdom; and that henceforth, denying all ungodliness and worldly lusts, you will live soberly, righteously and godly in this present world.

You do also cordially join yourselves to this church, and engage to submit to all its rules of government, to seek earnestly its peace, purity and edification, and to walk with all its members in charity and faithfulness, in meekness and sobriety. Do you thus freely and solemnly devote yourselves to be the Lord's?

[Members of the church here arise.]

RESPONSE OF THE CHURCH.

We, the members of this church, do cordially receive you as brethren and sisters beloved to our communion and fellowship, and promise to walk with you in love, and to watch over you, to instruct, counsel, admonish and cherish you, with all long-suffering, gentleness and love.

[Here the pastor, in the name of the church, will give the right hand of fellowship.]

SECTION IV.

Judiciary Rules.

[*See 5th Elementary Principle, and Constitution, Article XII.*]

1. A church, when it shall judge it expedient, may appoint a Judicial Committee, of not less than three persons, who shall remain in office one year, unless displaced by the church. This committee shall be a standing court, to hear all complaints, and to try all charges against any lay member of the church; provided, that the church shall have power to refer any case to a special committee, when they shall judge that to be the best way to secure the ends of justice. When the accused is a female, female committees may be appointed when it is requested by the accused party.

In all trials the Pastor shall preside; but when the Pastor shall be the plaintiff, or when the church shall have no Pastor, the church may appoint some other person to preside; and in case of its neglecting so to do, the committee shall select a chairman.

2. In all cases of personal offense between brethren, the direction of our Lord in Matt. xviii, 15–17, shall be pursued:

"Moreover, if thy brother shall tresspass against thee, go and tell him his fault between thee and him alone; if he shall hear thee, thou hast gained thy brother.

"But if he will not hear thee, then take with thee one or two more, that in the mouths of two or three witnesses every word may be established.

"And if he shall neglect to hear them, tell it unto the Church; but if he neglect to hear the Church, let him be unto thee as a heathen and a publican."

In default of pursuing the above course here recommended, no charge shall lie against any minister or member.

3. A secretary shall be appointed by the committee, to take down regular minutes of the evidence and proceedings of the trial; which, together with a copy of the decision, and all other documents belonging to the trial, shall be preserved by the Pastor, who shall furnish each of the parties with a copy of the decision, if required.

4. In all cases of trial, a bill shall be made out, setting forth the charge, or charges, with the specifications in writing, and a copy of the same shall be served up-

on the accused by the Chairman of the Court, or by the complainant, allowing the accused a reasonable time to prepare for trial, which shall not be less than ten days, unless by consent of the parties.

5. A complaint against any member of the church shall be presented to the Pastor; but if there be no Pastor, or if he neglect to attend to the complaint, the charges shall be presented to the Judicial Committee; and if there be no standing Judicial Committee, the charges shall be presented to the church at one of its meetiggs; and if, in the judgment of the church, the charge be of such a nature, and founded upon such probable evidence as to demand an investigation, they shall appoint the necessary committee for the trial of the case.

6. A complaint against a minister or preacher shall be presented to the Pastor of the charge, or in case the Pastor be the accused party, to the President of the Conference, or other minister, not belonging to the charge, who shall cite the accused to appear before a committee of at least three ministers, which he shall select, and acting as chairman, he shall proceed to try the case.

7. A complaint against an offending church shall be presented to the President

of the Conference, or in case he be the Pastor of the church accused, to any other minister, provided he belong to some other charge, who shall call a committee of five male members, to assemble at the place where said church holds its regular religious meetings, and shall preside during the trial. Before this committee, the church, having been duly summoned, shall appear by its representative. If the church shall be found guilty of having violated the Elementary Principles, or the Constitution, or any of our essential disciplinary regulations, the same shall be reported to the ensuing Annual Conference, before which the church may appear by its representative in self-defence, and if the decision of the committee be confirmed, the church shall be stricken from the list of churches on the Conference record.

8. The accused may object to any member of the committee, on account of his having prejudged the case, being prejudiced against the accused, or of being interested in the decision. The challenge may extend to any number equal to the original committee. The accused shall also be allowed to introduce and examine witnesses, and to be heard in self-defense, and to have the assistance of any minister or member of the church.

9. The chairman shall decide all questions of law that may be raised during the progress of any trial; but the committee shall, by a majority of votes, decide the guilt or innocence of the accused, and if he be convicted, they shall determine what punishment shall be awarded; reproof, suspension, deposition, or expulsion; and the executive minister shall carry the same into effect.

10. In all cases of trial, the court shall appoint a Secretary, who shall make a faithful record of the proceedings, and the chairman shall transmit the same, or a true copy thereof, in case of an appeal, to the church if it be a lay member, to the quarterly conference if it be a preacher, and to the Annual Conference if it be a minister.

11. Every person convicted before a committee, designing to appeal, shall signify, in writing, to the chairman of the committee, his intention to do so, within twenty days after the close of the trial, or his appeal shall not be entertained.

12. If any accused minister, preacher, or member evade trial by absenting himself, after due notice shall have been given him, the investigation before the committee shall, nevertheless, be instituted, and the testimony heard; and if a majority

of the committee find him guilty of the charge, or charges, the executive minister shall carry the sentence into effect.

13. On any dispute between two or more members of our Church, concerning the payment of debts, or otherwise, which cannot be settled by the parties concerned, the Pastor shall recommend to the contending parties a reference, consisting of one arbiter chosen by the plaintiff and another by the defendant; the two arbiters to choose a third, a majority of whom shall decide the case.

14. When any minister, preacher, or member of our Church fails in business, and applies for the benefit of the insolvent laws, and there be reason to believe that he has been guilty of dishonesty, or if he require an investigation, a committee shall be appointed as in other cases; and if there be evidence to said committee that there has been intentional fraud, the said minister, preacher, or member shall be dealt with as in other cases of immorality. Where it shall appear to the committee of inquiry that there is no proper ground of censure, the committee shall furnish a certificate of honorable acquittal.

SECTION V.

Leaders' Meeting.

1. In every station where there are two classes or more, there shall be held monthly a leader's meeting, composed of all the class leaders and stewards, together with the Pastor, who shall be chairman of the meeting.

2. Each meeting shall be opened with prayer. A secretary shall be appointed annually, or oftener if necessary, whose duty it shall be to make a fair record of the proceedings, in a book kept for that purpose.

3. The names of all the leaders and stewards shall be called over, noting those present or absent, and the amount each leader pays over to the stewards or treasurer, as weekly, monthly, or quarterly collections from his class.

4. The leaders' class-books shall be examined quarterly by the meeting.

5. The leaders' meeting shall occasionally inquire into the punctuality of each leader in meeting his class, visiting his sick and delinquent members, and his attendance at the leaders' meeting, and all

prudential means shall be employed to induce faithfulness in the discharge of these important duties.

6. Inquiry shall be made at each meeting for the sick, and those who may need a pastoral visit.

7. All appropriations for the relief of the poor in the station, shall be made by the leaders' meeting and applied by the stewards, who shall visit the suffering member or members, in company with the leader, and administer to their necessities in the manner prescribed by the meeting.

8. The stewards shall pay over to the Pastor, through their treasurer, the class collections, and all such other monies as may come into their hands as pastor's salary.

SECTION VI.

Quarterly Conference.

[*See Constitution, Article V.*]

1. The Quarterly Conference shall be called to order by the Pastor, when present, who shall preside; provided, the conference may appoint some other person to

preside when they shall judge it necessary. The conference shall appoint a Secretary, and a portion of Scripture shall be read and prayer offered before proceeding to business. One-third of all the members in stations, and one-sixth in circuits shall constitute a quorum.

2. Should a charge of immorality, neglect of Christian duty, or of disseminating unscriptural doctrines be preferred against any member of the conference during the examination, the accusation, together with the names of the accuser and witnesses, shall be referred to the proper authorities, to be investigated in accordance with the provisions of the Constitution and the Discipline. When a case is so referred, a prosecutor shall be appointed by the conference in behalf of the church.

3. The first quarterly conference in each conference year, shall appoint a committee of examination, to assist, advise, and examine candidates for the ministry. It shall be the duty of the committee to see that the candidates pursue the course of reading prescribed by the discipline; to examine them occasionally on doctrines and religious experience; and when they shall have made the necessary attainments, to give them a written testimonial of their qualifications. But no committee shall

give a testimonial unless the candidate be a man of unexceptionable moral character, genuine piety, and have respectable attainments; at least an ability to state and defend the leading doctrines of Christianity.

And after he shall have been licensed, he shall continue under the inspection of the committee of examination, in view of his ordination.

No person shall be licensed to preach except he present a testimonial from the committce of examination.

The following questions shall be put to each candidate, and if he answer them satisfactorily he may be licensed:

Have you faith in Christ, and are you striving to be holy in heart, and in all manner of conversation?

Have you any other motive in requesting license to preach, than a desire to be instrumental in edifying the Church of God, calling sinners to repentance, and saving your own soul and those that hear you?

Do you believe that the Holy Scriptures of the Old and New Testaments contain all things necessary to salvation?

Have you examined our constitution and discipline; do you approve of them, and are you willing to comply with their requirements?

Are you solvent?

4. The Quarterly Conference, with the advice and consent of the Pastor, shall have authority to make all necessary alterations in their circuit or station, and to provide for filling all the appointments during the interval of the Annual Conference.

5. The Quarterly Conference shall determine its place of meeting, and the Pastor shall appoint the time, and give due notice of the same, and may call special meetings when important business demands it.

6. The Quarterly Conference shall have authority, at its first session in each year, to appoint a standing Advisory Committee, of three or five, who shall assist the Pastor, by their advice and counsel, in all important acts of his administration; and with whom he shall consult, at least once a quarter, for the purpose of receiving such suggestions as they may deem necessary for the prosperity and success of the work.

7. In every case where a parsonage belongs to a circuit, the Quarterly Conference shall have authority to elect, or cause to be elected, trustees thereof, in accord-

ance with the statute laws of the State, to hold said property for the benefit of such circuit.

8. The Quarterly Conference, in conjunction with the Pastor, shall have authority to receive ministers and preachers from other denominations, on satisfactory testimonials.

9. In all appeals brought before the Quarterly Conference, the same order shall be observed, and the same priviliges accorded to the appellant and accuser, as are granted in appeals before the Annual Conference.

10. The following order of business is recommended to the Quarterly Conferences:—When the Conference shall have been organized, let the list of members be called over by the Secretary, noting those present and absent, after which the Chairman shall present the following questions and items:

(1.) Are there any objections to any members of the Quarterly Conference?

(2.) Are there any appeals pending?

(3.) Are there any applications for license to exhort; or any to renew? or for license to preach; or to renew?

(4.) Are there any to recommend for orders? or to serve under the stationing authority of the Annual Conference?

(5.) Are there any applications from ministers or preachers, to become members of this Quarterly Conference?

(6.) Are there any changes in the time and place for preaching desired?

(7.) Are there any additions to, or corrections of the register to make?

(8.) Who will you have for the Advisory Committee?

(9.) Who will you have for the Committee on Examination?

(10.) Where will you have your next Quarterly meeting?

(11.) Is there any incidental business?

(12.) Call for report of Stewards.

SECTION VII.

Annual Conference.

See Constitution, Article VI.

1. The Conference shall be called to order by the President of the preceding year, who shall open it by reading the Scriptures and prayer, and shall preside until a new President is elected. If the President is not present, the Conference shall appoint a President *pro tem*, who shall act

until the election. A Secretary shall be appointed, to serve during the sitting of the Conference, and until the ensuing Conference.

2. The Conference shall judge of election returns, and qualifications of the delegates, or alternates who have been elected to serve instead of the delegates. A majority of all the members in attendance shall constitute a quorum.

3. Should a charge of immorallity be preferred against any ministerial member of the Conference, during the examination of character, and if the Conference see sufficient reason to justify it, the accusation, together with the names of the accuser and witnesses, shall be referred to the President of the Conference, to be investigated by committee, in the circuit or station where the supposed offense is alleged to have been committed; and the Conference shall appoint a prosecutor in behalf of the church. When charges are preferred against a minister or preacher in the interval of Conference, the President shall appoint the prosecutor. The Annual Conferences respectively, shall provide for the payment of any expenses incurred in bringing committees from a distance, to take part in judicial investigations.

4. Ministers or preachers of the Meth-

odist Church, in order to be eligible to membership in an Annual Conference, must have a written recommendation from a quarterly conference, or a certificate from some other Annual Conference, or the President thereof. No minister shall be placed on the supernumerary or superannuated list, except by vote of the Annual Conference. Neither shall any minister be recognised as belonging to our body, whose name is not recorded on the list of some quarterly or Annual Conference, to which he is amenable, or who does not hold a valid certificate or legal transfer.

5. No conference shall have power to withhold a testimonial, if the minister or preacher requiring it shall have complied with his engagements, and his moral character stands fair; but neither the conference into which the minister or preacher wishes to be received, nor its President, shall be obliged to employ him as an itinerant or missionary, except his labors can be profitably directed.

6. Every minister or preacher received by the President, during the interval of Conference, shall be subjected to a vote of the Conference before his name can be printed in the minutes as a stationed min-

ister or preacher, except in cases of transfer.

7. Ministers laboring under the direction of the Conference may be transferred from one district to another, by negotiations between the Presidents of said districts; provided the minister or preacher consents to the transfer; and provided the instrument have the signature of both Presidents; and, provided also, that it be presented to the Annual Conference to which the minister or preacher is to be transferred before it shall have closed its session, next following the date of the transfer; otherwise it shall not be valid. The transfer, when made for a period not exceeding three years, shall be viewed as temporary; and if the minister or preacher return to his own Conference before or at the time specified, he shall, if his moral character stand fair, be again admitted to membership, and shall be entitled to all the privileges and claims he would have possessed, had he not been thus transferred. All ministers and preachers holding transfers, shall be responsible to the authorities of the Conference giving such transfer, until the transfer shall receive the signature of the President of the Conference to which he designs to make his application.

8. Ministers and preachers coming from other denominations may be received and employed by the Annual Conference, provided they present suitable testimonials of good standing; and, provided also, the Conference shall be satisfied with the faith, Christian experience and qualifications of the applicant. Any minister may retire from the service of the Conference, and be received back again without recommendation from the quarterly conference, if he make the application within three years; provided his moral character stands fair. An Annual Conference may leave a minister without an appointment, at his own request, the ensuing year. When any minister is so left, he shall be entitled to a seat in the quarterly conference where he may reside; but shall be ultimately responsible to the Annual Conference. A superannuated minister shall likewise have a seat in the quarterly conference of the circuit or station where he may reside, and be ultimately accountable to the Annual Conference.

This rule shall apply to Editors, Book Agents, Presidents of Colleges, Professors, etc., as well those living beyond the bounds of their Annual Conferences, as those living within the bounds thereof.

9. No minister or preacher who shall

have been rejected by an Annual Conference shall be employed by its President, unless the Conference grant him permission under specified conditions.

10. Every preacher shall be eligible to Elder's orders after he shall have preached two years under a license, provided that no applicant shall be elected to orders who shall not first undergo an examination by the committee on orders appointed by the Annual Conference; provided further, that when it is impracticable for the applicant to attend, of which the Annual Conference shall judge, the Annual Conference may appoint a committee of examination in his neighborhood or circuit, upon whose recommendation he may be ordained in the interval of the Annual Conference, as provided in the discipline; and provided further, that the examination shall precede the election, and that the President shall be chairman of the committee.

11. In cases of missions and similar necessities, preachers may be elected to elder's orders without regard to time, provided they possess the requisite qualifications.

12. No man shall be elected to Elder's orders, except he be a man of unexceptionable moral character, genuine piety, respectable attainments, and sound in the

belief of the fundamental doctrines of Christianity, and faithful in the discharge of gospel duties.

13. The elders shall have authority to administer the Lord's Supper, baptize, and celebrate matrimony, and perform all parts of divine worship.

14. Ordination shall be performed by the President, assisted by two or more other elders.

15. Every person who appeals to the Annual Conference, from a decision of a committee of trial, shall be permitted to appear before the Conference, and after all the documents belonging to the trial had before the committee shall have been read, shall state the reasons of his appeal. His accuser shall then be permitted to support his charges in the presence of the appellant. The appellant may in turn make his reply, which shall close the proceedings on both sides, except the Conference grant the accuser permission to speak a second time. The appellant and accuser shall then retire, and the Conference shall decide, and furnish the appellant with a copy of their decision. In all trials on appeals, the court shall not go beyond the record of the court below, but shall decide in view of the pleadings and evidence therein contained; unless the accused shall

have given notice at the time he signified his intention to appeal, that he should request the upper court to open the whole merits of the case, when new testimony may be introduced, and the court shall give its own and final decision in the case. When the appeal is tried upon the record of the court below, the decision shall acquit the accused, or confirm the judgment rendered below, or order a new trial. These rules shall apply to appeals to churches and quarterly conferences.

16. Each Annual Conference, respectively, shall have power to make its own rules and regulations in regard to stationing its ministers and preachers, provided it shall make no rule inconsistent with the Constitution of the Methodist Church.

17. It shall be the duty of the President of each Ahnual Conference, at each of its annual sessions, to call the attention of the Conference to the claims of the Missionary, Educational, and such other general interests of the Church as may properly come before them, for such action as may be deemed necessary.

18 The Conference shall divide the district into circuits and stations, change the boundaries of the same, and form new charges from year to year, as the interest of the work demands; provided, that no

station or circuit shall be divided, unless each part have ability to support one or more preachers, and the delegate or delegates from the circuit or station request the division.

19. The Conference shall not be required to appoint ministers and preachers to circuits and stations, who, in their opinion, are incompetent to the duties thereof, or who they believe will neglect the work, if it be assigned to them; and Conference may transfer such ministers and preachers to the unstationed list; provided this rule shall not authorize the Conference to transfer to the unstationed list, any who are entitled to a place on the superannuated list.

20. No minister or preacher, engaged to serve a circuit or station under the direction of the Conference, shall abandon his work before the expiration of his term of service, unless by consent of the President, who may release him for satisfactory reasons.

21. The Annual Conferences, respectively, shall elect annually a standing district committee of three elders, one of whom shall be an unstationed minister, and three laymen, whose duty it shall be, in the event of the death, resignation, or suspension of the President, to appoint a President *pro*

tem. to serve until the sitting of the next Annual Conference.

Should charges be preferred against the President of an Annual Conference, the committee shall call upon an elder residing in the district to perform the official notifications, and to act as executive officer in the trial, in accordance with the rule provided for the trial of ministers.

22. It shall be the duty of each minister and preacher engaged in regular pastoral work, to furnish annually to the steward of the Conference of which he is a member, a report of the amount of compensation received during the preceding year.

23. Each Annual Conference shall cause the following statistics to be reported from the various charges, each year: viz: Number of members; Number of probationers; Number received during the year; Number and value of Church edifices and parsonages; Number of Church periodicals taken; Number of Sabbath-schools, teachers and scholars; Number of volumes in S. S. Library; Amounts paid for benevolent purposes.

24. No member of Conference shall withdraw himself from its sittings without permission, until all the business shall have been transacted.

25. It shall be the duty of every minister belonging to the Annual Conference to attend its annual sessions, or if unable to attend, to inform the Conference by letter of said inability, and the causes thereof. Any minister who shall neglect the above duty shall be subject to the censure of the Conference; and, if persisted in for two years in succession, shall be liable to lose his membership in said Conference by a vote thereof.

26. When circumstances make it necessary, the Annual Conference may supply the place of the President in ordinations, by substitnting any other elder in his stead.

27. In all cases where an Annual Conference shall omit or decline to prescribe the mode for the election of delegates to the Annual Conference, the following shall de the rule:

In the stations, the election shall be by the members, under the direction of the stewards, who shall designate the time and place, and serve as judges of the election. Every election shall be by ballot, and be held at least ten days before the sitting of the Annual Conference. Notice shall be given on the preceding Sabbath, from the pulpit, or pulpits, of the time and place of holding the election. No person shall be declared elected except he have a majority of all the votes given.

In circuits, the delegates shall be elected by ballot, at the quarterly conference next preceding the sitting of the Annual Conference, under the direction of the stewards, who shall act as judges of the election. In this and other elections, and in settlement of all questions requiring a vote of the church, all members shall be entitled to vote.

28. We recommend the following, as the order of business to be observed in the Annual Conference:

1. When the Annual Conference shall have been organized, let the certificates of all the delegates be examined, and a complete list of all the members of the Conference be made out.

2. Elect the President for the ensuing year.

3. Appoint the following committees, and such others as may be deemed necessary:

(1.) A committee on boundaries of stations, circuits and missions.

(2.) A committee on Pastoral Relations, if such shall be agreed upon as per paragraph 16 of section vi.

(3.) A committee to examine candidates for orders, and persons recommended to be employed under the direction of the Conference.

(4.) A committee on religious services during the sitting of the Conference.

(5.) A committee on statistics.

(6.) A committee to prepare the minutes for publication, obituaries, etc.

(7.) The standing district committee.

4. Appoint a Conference Steward, and a committee to assist him, if any be judged necessary.

5. Examine the official conduct of all the ministers and preachers laboring under the direction of the Conference.

6. Receive ministers and preachers to be employed under the direction of the Conference.

7. Elect to orders.

8. Grant superannuated relations.

9. Receive and hear appeals from committees of trial.

10. Hear and act upon the report of the committee on pastoral relations.

11. Receive the general exhibit of the Conference Steward.

12. Call for the report of the committee on statistics.

13. Appoint the time and place for holding the succeeding Annual Confer-

ence; provided that when a President and standing committee, or a majority of them, shall be satisfied of the necessity of so doing, they may change the time or place for holding a succeeding Annual Conference, by giving public notice thereof in the district, at least three months previous to the time of holding such Conference.

If there be any unfinished business reported as standing on the past year's journal, it may be taken up under its proper head, or at any time the Conference may deem proper; and any incidental matter may be introduced after the regular business of the Conference shall have been completed.

14. Elect representatives to the General Conference.

Section VIII.

Advice to Ministers and Preachers.

Keep your own soul alive to God by meditation, prayer, and searching the scriptures daily. Read the Old and New Testaments regularly through, if practicable, once every year,; and avail yourself of all the helps within your reach, to obtain a correct understanding of the word of life. "Study to show thyself approved unto God, a workman that needeth not to be ashamed, rightly dividing the word of truth."

Neither be unemployed, nor engaged about trifles. Do everything at the time appointed, and complete everything you commence. Never disappoint a congregation, nor spend more time in a place than is strictly necessary. Labor constantly to feel the high responsibilities of your office and ministry; take heed that the blood of souls be not found on your skirts.

Be an example of the believers, in word, in conversation, in charity, in spirit, in faith, in purity; and avoid all affectation, effeminacy, and everything like austerity. Be affable and courteous in your manners; and let your whole deportment be mild and inoffensive. "Learn of me," said the blessed Jesus, "for I am meek and lowly in heart."

In your dress, keep clear of the two extremes, antiquated singularity on the one hand, and fashionable foppishness on the other. Abstain from the use of tobacco in all its forms; and use no spirituous liquors.

Remember, it is your imperious duty not to preach yourself, but Christ crucified, the great sacrifice for sin, and the only Savior of the world. We "charge thee, therefore, before God and the Lord Jesus Christ, who shall judge the quick and the dead, at his appearing; preach the word; be instant, in season, out of season; reprove, rebuke, exhort, with all ong sufferlng and doctrine."

SECTION IX.

General Conference.

1. The General Conference, at its quadrennial sessions, shall elect a Publishing, Missionary, Educational, and such other Boards as may properly come under its control; which Boards shall have full authority to adopt such measures as may be necessary to render them efficient in their several departments.

2. It shall also elect an Editor for its official organs, a Book Agent, and Corresponding Secretaries for the Missionary and Educational Boards—who shall report to and be amenable to the General Conference, for their official acts.

3. It shall be the duty of the Editor, Book Agent, and the Corresponding Secretaries of the above Boards, to meet semi-annually, or oftener, if necessary, for the purpose of mutual counsel and co-operation, in carrying forward the interests committed to their hands.

4. It shall be their duty, as far as is consistent with their direct official acts, to see that some one of their number visits each Annual Conference, for the purpose of presenting these general church interests for their consideration and action.

5. The President of the preceding General Conference, the Editor and Book Agent, shall be a standing committee, to change, if necessary, the place of holding the succeeding General Conference; and in case a change is made, three months notice of the same shall be given.

SECTION X.

Additional Duties of the President.

[*See Constitution, Article VII, Section* 2.]

When a President makes an exchange of a minister or preacher from one circuit, station or mission to another, it shall be his duty to give him a written certificate of said change, which shall be his passport to the new appointment. He shall also give a certificate of employment to ministers, preachers and missionaries, whom he may employ in the recess of the Conference, without which no minister, preacher, or missionary shall be recognized as regularly appointed.

SECTION XI.

Pastors.

1. It shall be the duty of pastors to preach the Word, administer the ordinances, execute the discipline, and faithfully discharge all the duties belonging to the ministerial and pastoral office.

2. To visit all the classes, at least once a quarter, if practicable, and see that they are duly and properly met by their respective leaders, and that the members regularly attend their classes; and to hold an election within the last quarter in each Conference year, for the choice of a leader, in each class of his circuit or station;

but should any class refuse or neglect to elect, the pastor shall then appoint a leader for said class.

3. To give due notice, from all the pulpits in his circuit or station, of the time and place of holding the ensuing quarterly conference.

4. To hold love feasts, general class-meetings, and appoint prayer-meetings.

5. To detain the society occasionally, after preaching, for the purpose of giving them such advice and exhortation as may be requisite.

6. To organize, as far as practicable, Sabbath-schools at each appointment within his charge, and report to the ensuing Annual Conference in full the statistics of his charge as required by the discipline.

7. To keep an exact record of all the members belonging to his station, circuit, or mission, and of the baptisms; and report the latter, with the names of all members in full membership, to the quarterly conference, and the numbers in society in his charge, to the Annual Conference.

8. To present to the people of his charge, sometime during the Conference year, the claims of the Missionary, Educational, and such other general interests as the General Conference shall authorize, from time to time; and he shall be held responsible for

the same in the examination of character.

9. To report quarterly, when practicable, to the President, the state of his circuit or station; and at the close of the year, to leave to his successor a plan of his charge.

10. To give certificates to those who desire to remove to another station, circuit or society. But no certificate shall be valid longer than six months after date, except unavoidable circumstances shall have put it out of the power of the holder to join within the above named period. All ministers, preachers and members holding certificates, shall be responsible to the authority whence the certificate was taken, until it shall have been deposited elsewhere.

No pastor shall withhold a certificate or testimonial from persons whose moral character stands fair. A suitable testimonial shall not be withheld from those who propose to withdraw from the fellowship of the Methodist Church.

SECTION XII.

Duties of Associate Pastors.

It shall be the duty of the associate pastor to preach statedly in all the appointments, and to aid the pastor in the general work of the Gospel in the charge to which he has been appointed.

SECTION XIII.

Duties of Unstationed Ministers.

It shall be the duty of every unstationed minister or preacher, to preach in all the appointments officially assigned to him, and to render all the ministerial assistance in his circuit or station he can, consistently with his other duties; provided always, that at the time of making out a plan, every unstationed minister and preacher shall have the privilege of stating explicitly the amount of service he can consistently perform.

SECTION XIV.

Duties of Class Leaders.

[*See Constitution, Article VIII.*]

It shall be the duty of each class leader—

1. To meet his class once a week, in order to instruct the members in the principles and duties of Christianity; to comfort them in affliction; to advise them in cases of difficulty; and to exhort them to diligence in doing and suffering the whole will of God. And it shall also be the duty of each member of the class to meet him at the stated time and place appointed for holding the class meeting.

2. To receive what they are willing to give toward the support of the ministry, and the poor,—when not otherwise provided for,—and urge upon the members of his class liberality in their contributions, and punctuality in payment; and to hand over the records of his class to his successor.

Each leader shall have the names of all

the members entered in a book or paper kept by him for the purpose, in which he shall note weekly the presence or absence of each member, and give each one credit on the book or paper for the amount contributed.

3. It shall also be the duty of each leader to attend the leaders' meeting, (if one be held,) to represent the state of his class; to pay over to the stewards what he has received; and to inform the pastor of any that are sick, or need a pastoral visit.

4. It shall be the duty of each leader to visit the sick, and those members who frequently absent themselves from the means of grace; and to promote the spiritual, temporal and eternal interests of those committed to his care.

5. It shall be the duty of each leader to report to the pastor all cases of neglect of duty or improper conduct on the part of the members of his class, which, in his opinion, require the exercise of discipline.

Class leaders should occasionally meet each other's classes, and also vary the exercises in those meetings, for the purpose of making them interesting, lively and spiritual.

It is recommended, whenever practicable, that no class exceed thirty in number, and that no class meeting continue longer than one hour.

SECTION XV.

Duties of Conference Stewards.

[*See Constitution, Article VIII.*]

1. We recommend that it be the duty of each conference steward to receive the money for making up deficiencies in support of efficient and superannuated ministers and preachers, their widows and children.

2. To pay out of the funds received to the preachers the sums contributed to make up their deficiencies, as contemplated by those individuals or societies whose liberality shall have prompted them to ald in this good work.

The funds held by the steward shall be equally divided among all the claimants, except where individuals or societies direct a specific appropriation of any part of their contributions. But no one shall receive more than is judged necessary for his support.

In settling with the preachers, the conference steward shall account with them for all books and newspapers received by them on account of the book agent and editor. He shall pay no preacher's traveling expenses to or from the Conference; these must be paid by the preachers themselves, and be refunded to them by the stewards of the stations, circuits or missions to which they may be appointed for the ensuing year.

The traveling expenses of the delegates ought to be met by the respective circuits and stations which send them up to Conference, if they demand reimbursement.

3. To make out an accurate exhibit, at Conference, showing:

1st. What each preacher has received from his circuit or station during the past year.

2d. The amount paid to each out of the funds received for the support of the preachers.

3d. The amount forwarded to Conference from each circuit, station and mission, as Conference collection, and the respective sums forwarded by individuals or societies.

Each Annual Conference shall defray the expenses of its representatives to the General Conference.

SECTION XVI.

Duties of Circuit and Station Stewards.

[*See Constitution, Article VIII.*]

1. It shall be the duty of the stewards of a station, circuit or mission, to receive and take an exact account of the ordinary church collections, and all funds raised for the support of the preacher in the charge; to pay the preacher quarterly, or oftener, if necessary, out of the funds received; to meet all contingent expenses; and to make an accurate return to the church, or quarterly conference, of their receipts and disbursements during each quarter, and a fair exhibit of the temporal condition of the station or circuit.

2. To make the necessary provision and preparation for the Lord's Supper, and love feast; to receive the collections made on those occasions, and all other moneys contributed for the relief of the poor; and to distribute those funds as occasion may require, according to their best judgment,

having special regard to those poor members who are the most necessitous and deserving. The stewards shall make a quarterly return to the society, or quarterly conference, of their collections and contributions for the poor, and the state of those funds.

3. To use all proper means to induce the members, and those who sit regularly under our ministry, to be liberal in their contributions.

The stewards shall keep a separate book for the purpose of entering the weekly, monthly, or quarterly donations made by those who are not members of the church.

4. To see that a Conference collection be taken up, some time in the last quarter, previous to the sitting of the Annual Conference, both in the classes and in the congregations. The whole collection, when made, shall be forwarded by the stewards to the conference steward.

Section XVII.

Of Securing Titles to Church Property.

The laws of the several States are so various that no specific rule can be given which will meet the requirements of the diversified Statutes under which Churches have to organize. The following General Rules, if attended to, will secure the end desired.

1. Before taking a deed, examine the laws of the State, and see that the Church or Society is organized, and Trustees appointed according to the requirements of the Statute.

2. Let the property be deeded to Trustees, in trust for that particular Church or Society, giving its corporate name in the deed.

SECTION XVIII.

General Duties of Trustees.

1. Trustees shall be elected annually by the members of the church or society, according to the Statutes of the State. It shall be the duty of the Trustees to hold the property of the individual church in trust for the use and benefit thereof; and to fill all vacancies occasioned in their board by death, resignation, or ceasing to be a member of the Methodist Church.

2. It shall be their duty to hold periodical meetings, and keep a fair and regular record of the transactions of their board, in a book provided for the purpose, which shall at all times be open for the inspection of members of the church.

3. To take care of the church property, furniture and premises, burial ground, etc.

4. The Trustees shall have power, when authorized by a majority of the members over the age of twenty-one years, assembled at a regular meeting for the purpose, to purchase, build, repair, lease, sell, rent, mortgage, or otherwise procure or dispose of property, and on no other condition or conditions whatever.

5. In case any station or society shall become extinct by death, removals, or otherwise, the church property, if any, shall vest in the quarterly conference of the circuit, station or mission, or the Annual Conference, where there shall be no quarterly conference, to be disposed of in erecting meeting-houses for the benefit of the general body, after paying any debt that may exist against said society.

Section XIX.

Of Public Worship.

To establish uniformity among the churches, in public worship on the Lord's day, it is recommended that the following order be observed:

Let the morning service consist of:— 1. Singing; 2. Prayer, closing with the Lord's prayer; 3. Reading the Scriptures; 4. Singing; 5. Preaching; 6. Prayer; 7. Singing; 8. Benediction.

Let the afternoon or evening services be the same, with the exception that the reading of the Scriptures may be omitted. Or a social meeting may be held if preferred.

It is believed that kneeling is the most becoming attitude in time of prayer.

It is recommended that notices be given immediately before the preaching.

SECTION XX.

Means of Grace.

The means of grace recognized by the Methodist Church are, public worship, searching the Scriptures, the Lord's Supper, Love Feasts, Class meetings, private and family prayer.

Members of the church who neglect these means should be first labored with by the Leader and Pastor, and if they do not reform, they should be dealt with according to the fifth Elementary Principle and the Judiciary Rules.

SECTION XXI.

The Lord's Supper.

Order for the Administraiion of the Lord's Supper.

On the day appointed for the celebration

of the Lord's Supper, an appropriate discourse shall be delivered; after which, a collection shall be taken up for the relief of the poor.

While the stewards are making the collection, let the minister repeat one or more of the following passages:

Let your light so shine before men, that they may see your good works, and glorify your Father which is in heaven. Matt. v. 16.

He that soweth sparingly, shall also reap sparingly; and he that soweth bountifully, shall also reap bountifully. Let every man do according as he is disposed in his heart; not grudgingly, or of necessity; for God loveth a cheerful giver. 2 Cor. ix. 6, 7.

Charge those who are rich in this world, that they be ready to distribute, willing to communicate; laying up in store for themselves a good foundation against the time to come, that they may lay hold on eternal life. 1 Tim. vi. 17—19.

Whoso hath this world's goods, and seeth his brother hath need, and shutteth up his bowels of compassion from him, how dwelleth the love of God in him? 1 John, iii. 17.

Blessed is he that considereth the poor; the Lord will deliver him in the time of trouble. Psalm xli. 1.

As we have therefore opportunity, let us do good unto all men, and especially unto them who are of the household of faith. Gal. vi. 10.

In the commencement of the communion service, the officiating minister or ministers shall repair to the table, nncover the elements, and address the communicants in the following words:

Dearly beloved, while we were yet sinners Christ died for us, and became the propitiation for our sins, and not for ours only, but for the sins of the whole world. In the same night he was betrayed he did institute this ordinance, and commanded his followers to continue the same in commemoration of his death, until he come again. You, therefore, who are striving to walk in all of his commandments blameless, will now accompany us in a petition to the throne of grace, that we may worthily commemorate the death and passion of our Lord and Savior Jesus Christ.

Let us pray.

Almighty God, our heavenly Father, who of thy tender mercy didst give thine only son Jesus Christ to suffer death upon the cross for our redemption; who there, by the oblation of himself, once offered, did make an atonement for the sins af the whole world; and did institute this ordinance, and in his holy gospel command us to continue a perpetual memory of his precious death, until his coming again; we pray thee to grant us grace, that while we partake of these symbols of the broken body and shed blood of our Lord Jesus Christ, in remembrance of his death and passion, we may, by faith in him, receive the remission of our sins and the salvation of our souls.

We are not worthy, O Lord, to gather up the crumbs from under thy table, for we have sinned and come short of thy glory; we have erred and strayed from thy ways like lost sheep; we have left undone those things which we ought to have done; and we have done those things which we ought not to have done. Have mercy on us, O God, our heavenly Father, forgive our sins, and restore unto us the joy of thy salvation, through Jesus Christ, who hath redeemed us by his own precious blood.

Almighty aud most merciful God we do not presume to approach this thy table, trusting in our own righteousness, but in the blood and righteousness of our Lord Jesus Christ, who, in the same night he was betrayed, took bread, and when he had given thanks, he brake it, and gave to his disciples, saying, take, eat; this is my body which was broken for you: this do in remembrance of me. After the same manner he took the cup, and when he had supped, said: this cup is the new testament in my blood, drink ye all of it. This do ye, as oft as you drink it, in remembrance of me.

Grant unto us, O our heavenly Father, the effectual assistance or thy holy Spirit, that while we partake of these thy creatures of bread and wine, according to thy Son our Saviour's holy institution, in grateful remembrance of his death and passion, that our hearts may be penetrated with unfeigned love and gratitude for the unspeakable gift of thy Son, in the redemption and salvation of our souls. May we be melted into tenderness on account of the great love wherewith Christ hath loved us, and given himself for us. May we ever remember his agony and bloody sweat in the garden of Gethsemane; his cruel mockings and scourgings in Pilate's hall; and his ignominious death on the cross. Surely he hath borne our griefs, and carried our sorrows; he was wounded for our transgressions, he was bruised for our iniquities, the chastisement of our peace was upon him, and by his stripes we are healed. May we have redemption through his blood which was shed for the remission of our sins, and being justified by faith in him, may be filled with love, have grace too keep all thy commandments, and show forth the Lord's death till he come. And finally, be brought, with all the Israel of God, to inherit eternal life, through the merits and mediation of our Lord and Saviour Jesus Christ. Amen.

The officiating minister or ministers may then give the following invitation:

Ye that do truly and earnestly repent of your sins, and are in love and charity with your neighbors, and intend to lead a new life, following the commandments of God, and walking from henceforth in his holy ways, draw near in faith, and partake of this ordinance to your comfort.

The ministers shall then distribute the bread to the communicants, saying:

Take, eat this in remembrance that Christ's body was broken for you; for while we were yet sinners Christ died for us, and became the propitiation for our sins, and not for ours only, but for the sins of the whole world.

While the ministers are passing the bread

around, they may repeat one or more of the following passages:

God so loved the world, that he give his only begotton Son, that whosoever believeth on him might not perish, but have everlasting life.

God sent not his Son into the world to condemn the world, but that the world through him might be saved.

Herein is love, not that we loved God, but that he loved us, and sent his Son to be the propitiation for our sins. If God so loved us we ought to love one another.

Christ loved the church, and gave himself for it. If ye love me, keep my commandments.

Not every one that saith unto me, Lord, Lord, shall enter into the kingdom of heaven; but he that doeth the will of my Father which is in heaven.

Blessed is he that shall eat bread in the kingdom of God.

The ministers shall likewise take of the wine, and give to each communicant, saying:

Drink ye all of this, in grateful remembrance, that the blood of Christ was shed for you; for ye were not redeemed with corruptible things, but with the precious blood of Christ; in whom we have redemption, through faith, even the forgiveness of our sins, and the sanctification of our souls.

While passing the wine round, the ministers may repeat one or more of the following passages:

If we confess our sins, he is faithful and just to forgive our sins, and to cleanse us from all unrighteousness.

If we walk in the light, as he is in the light, we have fellowship one with another, and the blood of Jesus Christ his Son, cleanseth us from all unrighteousness.

Unto him that loved us, and washed us from our sins in his own blood, and hath made us kings and priests unto God and his Father, be glory and dominion forever. Amen.

When all have partaken, what remains of the elements shall be placed upon the table, and covered with a fair linen cloth; and the service shall be concluded with extempore prayer, and the apostolical benediction.

The Lord's Supper should be administered at least once a month in stations, and so often in circuits, as to give an opportunity to all the members of partaking once a quarter.

On these solemn occasions let there be no hurry, no confusion. Let meditation, prayer, and gratitude to God for the unspeakable gift of his Son, occupy every soul.

While administering the Supper, one of the ministers should occasionally give out an appropriate verse or two of a hymn, to be sung by the congregation. This might be so timed as to serve for a signal for those who have communed, to rise and retire to their places in the church, and give opportunity for the remaining communicants to repair to the table.

Let those who have scruples concerning the receiving the Lord's Supper kneeling, be permitted to receive it either sitting or standing.

Section XXII.

Baptism of Infants.

When the child to be baptized is brought before the minister, he shall say to the parents:

Beloved friends, you are about to dedicate your beloved child to the service of the living and true God, who hath said: "Behold, all souls are mine, as the soul of the father is mine, so also the soul of the son is mine;" and the promise of acceptance and salvation is to you and your children and to all that are afar off. By this act you acknowledge the high claim of Almighty God to the life and services of your offspring; and your own obligations to the Most High, to your infant, and to the church of Christ, to guide its feet into the paths of righteousness, and to raise it up in the nurture and admonition of the Lord.

You will need all the wisdom and grace you can acquire, to enable you to discharge this your imperative duty; we therefore exhort you to pray to God constantly, so to enlighten your minds and influence your hearts, that you may, both by precept and example, be enabled to lead your children in the true and right way, and induce them to glorify God, in their souls and bodies, which is their reasonable service.

Let us pray.

Almighty and most merciful God, father of our spirits, former of our bodies, Redeemer and Savior of our souls, we thank thee that thou hast made it our privilege to dedicate our children to thy service, that they may be lively members of the Church of Christ, and heirs of eternal life.

We beseech thee, O our heavenly Father, to bestow upon the parents of this child, grace whereby they may serve thee acceptably, with reverence and godly fear, in holiness and righteousness all the days of their lives; that by precept and example they may train their child in all godly discipline and admonition, that it may be a worthy member of the Church of Christ. Grant, O Lord, that this child may die unto sin, and live unto righteousness, and being steadfast in faith, joyful through hope, and rooted in love, may safely pass the waves of this transitory life, and finally come to the haven of eternal repose, there to dwell with thee, world without end, through Jesus Christ our Lord.

Almighty God, grant that whosoever is dedicated to thee, by our office and ministry, may be indued with heavenly virtues, and ever remain in the number of thy faithful children, and be made a partaker of eternal life through thy mercy, O blessed Lord God, who dost live and govern all things, world without end. Amen.

The people shall then stand up, and the minister shall say:

They brought young children to Christ, that he should touch them, and his disciples rebuked those who brought them; but when Jesus saw it he was much displeased, and said, Suffer little children to come unto me, and forbid them not; for of such is the kingdom of God. Verily, I say unto you, whosoever shall not receive the kingdom of God as a little child, shall not enter therein.

And he took them up in his arms, put his hands upon them and blessed them.

The minister shall then take the child in his arms, and say to the friends of the child:

Name this child.

Repeating the name as given by the parents, he shall say, when baptizing:

N. I baptize thee in the name of the Father, and of the Son, and of the Holy Ghost. The Lord bless this child and grant *him* eternal life.

The minister shall then conclude with the apostolical benediction.

Infant baptism should be administered

monthly in all our churches, and oftener when necessary.

In infant baptism let it be an invariable rule to require the attendance of the parents of the child.

Let every adult person, and the parents of every child to be baptized, have the choice of immersion, sprinkling, or pouring.

Parents whose children have been baptized, should attend after service, and inform the minister of the age, &c., of the child, or children baptized, that he may enter their names, &c., on the church register.

SECTION XXIII.

Ministration of Baptism

TO SUCH AS ARE OF RIPER YEARS.

When the persons to be baptized present themselves, the minister shall say:

Dearly beloved, forasmuch as all men are born in sin, and that our Savior Christ saith, none can enter the kingdom of God, except he be regenerated and born anew, of water and of the Holy Ghost, I beseech you to call upon God the Father, through our Lord Jesus Christ, that of his bounteous goodness he will grant to these persons, now to be baptized, that which by nature they cannot have, and that they may be made lively members of the church of Christ, and heirs of eternal life.

The minister shall then demand of each of the persons to be baptized, severally:

1. Do you believe in the existence of God, and that he is a rewarder of all those who diligently seek him? I do.
2. Do you believe that the Lord Jesus Christ is the Redeemer and Savior of the world? I do.
3. The Sacred Scriptures inform us, that we have all sinned, and come short of the glory of God; but that if we confess our sins, he is faithful and just to forgive us our sins, and to cleanse us from all unrighteousness. Are you now determined, by the aid of divine grace, to forsake every evil way, to look to Christ as your only and all-sufficient Savior, and to walk in all the commandments of God? I am.
4. It is made our duty to search the Sacred Scriptures, and to attend on all the ordinances of the house of God; will you

endeavor to be faithful in the discharge of these duties?

I will, by the assistance of God's Holy Spirit.

Let us pray.

Almighty, everlasting God, whose most dearly beloved Son, Jesus Christ, for the forgiveness of our sins, did shed out of his most precious side both water and blood, and gave commandment to his disciples that they should go, teach all nations, and baptize them in the name of the Father, and of the Son, and of the Holy Ghost. Regard, we beseech thee, the supplications of this congregation; and grant that the persons now to be baptized may receive the fullness of thy grace, and ever remain in the number of thy elect children, through Jesus Christ our Lord.

O merciful God, grant, through the sanctification of thy spirit, and their belief of the truth, as it is in Christ Jesus, that the carnal mind in them may be destroyed, and that they may be created anew in Christ Jesus, unto good works, and have their fruit unto holiness, and obtain everlasting life.

Grant that they, being dedicated to thee, by our office and ministry, may receive grace whereby they may serve thee acceptably with reverence and godly fear, in holiness and righteousness all the days of their lives; and being indued with heavenly virtues, and strengthened by thy grace, may have victory, and be eventually rewarded, through thy mercy, O blessed Lord God, who dost live and govern all things, world without end. Amen.

The minister shall then ask the name, and then repeating the name, sprinkle or pour water upon him, (or her,) saying:

N. I baptize thee in the name of the Father, and of the Son, and of the Holy Ghost.

The minister may then conclude with *extempore* prayer, repeat the Lord's prayer, and the apostolical benediction.

Section XXIV.

Marriage Ceremony.

At the time appointed for solemnization of matrimony, the persons to be married, standing together, the man on the right hand, and the woman on his left, the minister shall say:

We are assembled in the presence of God and before these witnesses, to solemnize the marriage of these two persons present.

If any one can show just cause, why they may not lawfully be joined together, let him now speak, or else hereafter hold his peace.

The minister shall then address himself to the persons about to be married, and say:

If either of you know any lawful cause, or just impediment, why you may not legally be joined together in matrimony, I charge you to confess it; for no ceremony can make valid an unlawful marriage.

If no impediment be alleged, the minister, addressing himself to the parties, shall say:

Under the influence of mutual affection, you are now about to pledge your vows. It will be your mutual concern, to perpetuate your love by constant fidelity, and by a practical regard of those principles and rules of conduct which the word of God, and good experience, have furnished. Husband and wife should be studiously attentive to know each other's dispositions, and anticipate each other's wishes. Mutual tenderness and forbearance are indispensable to matrimonial happiness; nothing endears like these; nothing so effectually rivets affection.

The husband should consult his wife, make her acquainted with the true state of his affairs, and allow her a full share of influence; your interests will be one, and your confidence should be mutual.

The wife should love her husband, show him all possible attention, and make her house the place of his delight.

Husband and wife should conduct toward each other with the utmost affability, kindness and affection; and constantly seek the protection and assisting grace of God, to enable them faithfully and mutually to discharge the numerous and important duties required of those who become heads of families.

The minister shall then say:

Please join your right hands.

Then shall the minister say to the man:

Wilt thou have this woman to thy wedded wife, to love, comfort, honor, and keep her in sickness and in health; and forsaking all others, keep thee only unto her, so long as you both shall live?

The man shall answer:

I will.

Then shall the minister say unto the woman:

Wilt thou have this man to thy wedded husband, to obey, love, honor, and keep him in sickness and in health; and forsaking all others, keep thee only unto him, so long as you both shall live?

The woman shall answer:

I will.

The minister shall then say:

Let us pray.

We humbly supplicate thy blessing, heavenly Father, on these persons who have mutually entered into marriage covenant. Will it please thee to grant them power to keep their vows in fidelity; to live together in peace and love, and reverently obey thy laws. Under thy protection, and in the enjoyment of thy favor, may they long live in health and comfort, gratefully receiving all thy blessings which thy parental care and goodness may confer upon them in this life; and in the end, vouchsafe to them, and to us all, a participation in life everlasting. Amen.

Then shall the minister say:

Those whom God hath joined together, let no man put asunder.

Forasmuch as A. B. and C. D. have consented together in holy wedlock, and have witnessed the same before God and this company, and thereto have pledged their faith, the one to the other, and have declared the same by joining hands, I pronounce them husband and wife, in the name of the Father, and of the Son, and of the Holy Ghost. Amen.

SECTION XXV.

Burial of the Dead.

When the corpse is brought to the grave

the minister shall repeat one or more of the following passages:

I am the resurrection and the life, saith the Lord; he that believeth in me, though he were dead, yet shall he live; and whosoever liveth and believeth in me, shall never die.

I know that my Redeemer liveth, and that he shall stand at the latter day upon the earth; and though after death worms destroy this body, yet in my flesh shall I see God.

I heard a voice from heaven, saying unto me, Write; From henceforth, blessed are the dead who die in the Lord; even so saith the Spirit, for they rest from their labors, and their works do follow them.

Blessed be the God, and father of our Lord Jesus Christ, who, according to his abundant mercy, hath begotten us again unto a lively hope, by the resurrection of Jesus Christ from the dead, to an inheritance, incorruptible, undefiled, and that fadeth not away, reserved in heaven for those who are kept by the power of God through faith unto salvation, ready to be revealed at the last time.

Behold, I show you a mystery; We shall not all sleep, but we shall all be changed, in a moment, in the twinkling of an eye, at the last trump; for the trumpet shall sound, and the dead shall be raised incorruptible, and we shall be changed; for this corruptible must put on incorruption, and this mortal must put on immortality. So when this corruptible shall have put on incorruption and this mortal shall have put on immortality, then shall be brought to pass the saying that is written: Death is swallowed up in victory. O death, where is thy sting? O grave, where is thy victory? The sting of death is sin; and the strength of sin is the law; But thanks be to God, who giveth us the victory, through our Lord Jesus Christ.

Here the minister, if he judge proper, may exhort those present to reflect on the shortness and uncertainty of human life; and to prepare for death, judgment, and eternity.

Let us pray.

Almighty and most merciful God, in whose hands are the issues of life and death; and before whose bar we shall all stand, and give an account of the deeds done in the body; we beseech thee to grant unto us, at all times, a salutary conviction of the frailty of life, and our great responsibility to thee, the judge of quick and dead.

In the midst of life we are in death; we come up and are cut down like a flower; we flee as a shadow, and never continue in one stay. Death, judgment and eternity are just before us, and of whom may we seek protection and grace but of thee, O most merciful God, who hath redeemed us with the most precious blood of Christ, that we might be delivered from the power of sin and the fear of death, and be made heirs of eternal life.

We humbly confess, O righteous Father, that we have sinned, and come short of thy glory. We have been undutiful children, slothful servants, and unfaithful stewards of the manifold mercies of God. Be merciful, O Lord, to our unrighteousness; pardon our sins, and raise us from a death of sin to a life of righteousness, through faith in our Lord Jesus Christ, who hath said, I am the resurrection and the life; he that believeth in me, though he were dead, yet shall he live; and whosoever liveth and believeth in me shall not die eternally.

We beseech thee, Father of all our mercies, and giver of every good and perfect gift, to grant us grace whereby we may serve thee acceptably, with reverence and godly fear, all our days; looking for the blessed hope, and glorious appearing of the great God and our Savior Jesus Christ, to judge the world in righteousness. For the hour is coming, in which all that are in their graves shall hear the voice of the Son of God, and shall come forth; they that have done good, to the resurrection of life, and they that have done evil, to the resurrection of condemnation.

Forbid, O most merciful God, that any of us should taste of the bitter pains of the second death; but grant that when we depart this transitory life, we may die in possession of triumphant faith, and rest in Christ. And, at the general resurrection of the last day, be found acceptable in thy sight, and receive that blessing which thy well beloved Son shall pronounce to all that love and fear thee; saying, Come, ye blessed of my Father, receive the kingdom prepared for you from the beginning of the world.

Almighty God, our heavenly Father, grant that this dispensation of thy righteous providence may be sanctified to the good of all present. May we take due warning and consider the shortness and uncertainty of human life; the solemnities of death, and the awful realities of eternity; and prepare to meet thee in the judgment.

May the relatives of the deceased not sorrow as those who have no hope, but have grace to submit to thy gracious will, and be fully prepared to say—the Lord gave and the Lord hath taken away; blessed be the name of the Lord.

Benediction.

The grace of our Lord Jesus Christ, the love of God, and the fellowship of the Holy Spirit remain with us, now and forever. Amen.

When the corpse is deposited in the grave, and the sexton is returning the earth, the minister may repeat one or more of the following passages:

Dust thou art, and unto dust thou shalt return.

It is appointed unto men once to die, and after that the judgment.

Blessed and holy are they who have part in the first resurrection. On such the second death hath no power; but they shall be priests of God and of Christ, and shall reign with him forever. God will wipe all tears from their eyes; and there shall be no more death; neither sorrow nor weeping; neither shall there be any more pain; for the former things have passed away.

Eye hath not seen, nor ear heard, neither have entered into the heart of man, the things which God hath prepared for them that love him.

Blessed are they that keep his commandments, that they may have a right to the tree of life, and may enter in through the gates into the city.

Precious in the sight of the Lord is the death of his saints.

SECTION XXVI.

Form and Manner of Ordaining Elders.

On the day of ordination a sermon or exhortation shall be delivered; after which one of the elders shall read aloud the names of the persons to be ordained, who shall answer respectively, and present themselves before the ministers appointed to perform the ordination.

One of the Elders shall then read the following passages of Holy Writ:

"And Jesus came, and spake unto them, saying, All power is given unto me in heaven and in earth. Go ye, therefore, and teach all nations; baptizing them in the name of the Father, and of the Son, and of the Holy Ghost. Teaching them to observe all things whatsoever I nave commanded you; and lo, I am with you always, even unto the end of the world. Amen." Matt. xxviii, 18-20.

"But unto every one of us is given grace according to the measure of the gift of Christ. Wherefore he saith, when he ascended up on high, he led captivity captive, and gave gifts unto men. Now that he ascended, what is it but that he also descended first into the lower parts of the earth? He that descended is the same also that ascended up far above all heavens, that he might fill all things. And he gave some apostles, and some prophets, and some evangelists, and some pastors and teachers. For the perfecting of the saints, for the work of the ministry, for the edifying of the body of Christ. Till we all come in the unity of the faith, and of the knowledge of the Son of God, unto a perfect man, unto the measure of the stature of the fullness of Christ." Ephesians iv. 7-13.

"This is a true saying, if a man desire the office of a bishop, he desireth a good work. A bishop then must be blameless, the husband of one wife, vigilant, sober, of good behavior, given to hospitality, apt to teach. Not given to wine, no striker, not given to filthy lucre; but patient; not a brawler, not covetous. One that ruleth well his own house; having his children in subjection with all gravity. (For if a man know not how to rule his own house, how shall he take care of the church of God?) Not a novice, lest being lifted up with pride, he fall into the condemnation of the devil. Moreover, he must have a good report of them which are without, lest he fall into reproach, and the snare of the devil." 1 Tim. iii. 1–7.

Another of the elders shall say to the persons about to be ordained:

Beloved brethren, forasmuch as the holy scriptures command that we should not be hasty in laying on of hands, and admitting persons to minister in the church of Christ; therefore, before we admit you to the office of elder in the church of God, we will examine you in the presence of this congregation, and receive your answers to the following questions:

Are you fully persuaded that the holy scriptures contain sufficiently all doctrine required of necessity for eternal salvation?

And will you out of the same holy scriptures instruct the people, and teach and maintain nothing, as of necessity required for salvation, but that which you shall be persuaded may be proved by them?

Will you faithfully exercise yourself in the study of the holy scriptures, and call upon God, by prayer, for the true understanding of the same, so that you may be able to teach and exhort with wholesome doctrine, and to withstand and convince gainsayers?

Will you deny all ungodliness and worldly lusts, and live soberly, righteously, and godly in this present world, that you may show yourself in all things a worthy example to the flock of Christ?

Will you diligently endeavor to teach and discipline your family according to the doctrine of the gospel, and make them, as much as in you lieth, examples to others?

Will you strive to maintain quietness, peace and love among all christian people, and especially among them who are committed to your care?

Let us pray.

All shall now kneel before God, and the elder shall say:

Almighty God, giver of every good and perfect gift, mercifully behold these thy servants now set apart for the office and work of elders in thy church. Grant so to replenish them with the truth of thy doctrine, and adorn them with innocency of life, that both by word and good example, they may faithfully serve the church in this office, to the glory of thy name, and the edification of thy people, through the merits of our Savior Jesus Christ. Amen.

The elders present shall then lay their hands severally upon the head of every one that receiveth the order of elder, the receivers remaining on their knees, for the convenience of the ordainers:

The president pronouncing aloud the following words:

The Lord pour upon thee the Holy Spirit for the office and work of an elder, committed unto thee by the election of thy brethren, and the imposition of our hands; and be thou faithful.

The president shall then deliver to each one the Bible in his hands, saying:

We acknowledge thy authority to preach this word, and to administer the ordinances in the church of Christ.

Feed the flock of God, taking the oversight thereof; not as a lord over God's heritage, but being an example to the flock. And when the chief Shephard shall appear, thou shalt receive a crown of glory that fadeth not away.

Then shall the President say:

Let us pray.

Most merciful Father, we beseech thee to grant unto these thy servants, now set apart to the office of elder, thy heavenly blessing; and so indue them with thy Holy Spirit, that they, preaching thy word, may not only be earnest to reprove, beseech, and exhort, with all patience and long suffering; but also may be, to such as believe, wholesome example, in doctrine, in conversation, in love, in faith, in charity, in purity; that faithfully fulfilling their course, at the last day, each one may receive a crown of righteousness, laid up by the Lord, the righteous Judge, who liveth and reigneth one God with the Father and the Holy Ghost, world without end.

Assist us, O Lord, in all our doings, with thy most gracious favor, and further us with thy continued help; that in all our works, begun, continued and ended in thee, we may glorify thy holy name; and finally, by thy mercy obtain everlasting life, through Jesus Christ our Lord. Amen.

Benediction.

The peace of God, which passeth understanding, keep your hearts and minds in the knowledge and love of God, and of his Son Jesus Christ our Lord, and the blessing of God Almighty, the Father, the Son and the Holy Ghost, be with you always. Amen.

SECTION XXVII.

Boundaries of Respective Districts.

MAINE DISTRICT,

Includes all the State of Maine.

BOSTON DISTRICT,

Includes all the States of Massachusetts, Rhode Island, and New Hampshire.

NEW YORK DISTRICT.

The New York District shall include the States of Vermont and Connecticut, and that part of the State of New York lying east of a line forming the boundary between the States of New York and New Jersey, terminating at the Delaware river; thence up said river to the north-west corner of Sullivan county; thence north to the north-east corner of Hamilton county;

thence east to Lake Champlain; thence down the Lake to the Canada line.

NEW JERSEY DISTRICT,

Includes the State of New Jersey, and the city of Philadelphia.

ONONDAGA DISTRICT,

Commences at the point where the old pre-emption line intersects Lake Ontario, and runs thence southwardly, bounding on the Genesee District, to the line of the Pennsylvania District; thence along said line, so far as to embrace Cherry Valley and Westford Circuits, and all the territory west and south of the county of St. Lawrence, (with the exception of Twin Circuit;) thence, in a north-westwardly direction, to the Oswego river; and thence by Lake Ontario to the place of beginning.

GENESEE DISTRICT,

Commences at the point where the old pre-emption line intersects Lake Ontario, and runs thence, in a direct line, to the foot of Seneca Lake; thence up the middle of said lake to the line of the Pennsylvania District; thence west, to the north-west corner of said district; thence south, to the southern boundary line of the State of New York; thence, by said State line, to Lake Erie, and thence, by said lake, the Niagara river, and Lake Ontario, to the place of beginning.

PENNSYLVANIA DISTRICT,

Begins at the junction of the Lehigh and Delaware rivers, and runs thence, by a direct line, to Harrisburg, (including that city;) thence, by the Susquehanna river, to the mouth of the Juniata; thence up the Juniata to the dividing line of Mifflin and Huntington counties; thence, by a direct line due north, into Allegheny county (New York) so far as to embrace Broome county by a line due east, thence by the north-east and east lines of Broome county to the Delaware, and thence, by said river, to the place of beginning.

PITTSBURGH DISTRICT,

Includes that portion of the State of Pennsylvania lying west of the Allegheny mountains, together with Clearfield Circuit, formerly belonging to the Maryland District, and that portion of the State of Ohio lying east of the Cleveland and Pittsburg rail-road, except Cleveland, Wellsville and Liverpool, which shall belong to the Muskingum District.

WEST VIRGINIA DISTRICT,

Includes all of West Virginia, and the adjacent parts of Kentucky, except that all the portion of the Pan Handle (so called) lying north of Wheeling and of the National Road, belongs to the Pittsburgh District, as also Morgantown Mission.

MUSKINGUM DISTRICT,

Includes all that part of the State of Ohio not included in the Ohio and Pittsburgh Districts.

OHIO DISTRICT,

Includes that part of the State of Ohio lying west of the Sciota and Sandusky rivers, excepting the counties of Crawford Seneca, Sandusky and Wyandott.

MICHIGAN AND WESTERN MICHIGAN DISTRICTS.

In October, 1858, the Michigan District, by unanimous consent, was divided, upon the following plan:

"A new district was set off, the line being as follows: All west of the meridian line in Michigan, and the northern tier of counties of the State of Indiana, with Adrian and Monroe Circuits, and all of Jackson county, in Michigan. Adrian and

Monroe Circuits to belong to Michigan Conference.

INDIANA AND WABASH DISTRICTS.

The division line to be the Cumberland road, from the Ohio State line to Indianapolis; thence west with the road leading through Danville, Rockville, and Montezuma, to the Illinois State line; the north part to be called the Wabash District. and the southern part to be called the Indiana District; towns on the line to be embraced in the Wabash District.

NORTH ILLINOIS DISTRICT,

Shall include all that part of the State of Illinois lying north of the Great Western railroad.

SOUTH ILLINOIS DISTRICT,

Embraces all that portion of the State of Illinois lying south of the Great Western railroad.

IOWA DISTRICT.

The Iowa District shall embrace all that part of the State of Iowa lying south of a line commencing with the intersection of the correction line and Mississippi river, in Scott county; running due west with said line to the west line of Poweshiek and Jasper counties; thence due west to the Missouri river.

NORTH IOWA DISTRICT.

The North Iowa District includes all the State of Iowa not included in the Iowa District.

WISCONSIN DISTRICT,

Includes the State of Wisconsin.

MINNESOTA DISTRICT,

Includes the State of Minnesota.

MISSOURI DISTRICT,

Shall include that part of the State of Missouri lying south of the Missouri river.

NORTH MISSOURI DISTRICT,

Shall include all that part of the State of Missouri lying north of the Missouri river.

NEBRASKA DISTRICT,

Shall include the State of Nebraska.

KANSAS DISTRICT,

Shall include the State of Kansas.

CALIFORNIA DISTRICT,

Shall include the State of California.

OREGON DISTRICT,

Shall include the State of Oregon, and Washington Territory.

NORTH CAROLINA DISTRICT,

Shall include the State of North Carolina.

It is recommended that all the territory not embraced in the above Conferences, be considered missionary ground, open for cultivation, in view of forming missions, circuits, and Annual Conferences; and that within the bounds of any State not included in the limits of an Annual Conference of the Methodist Church, any number of local churches, receiving our faith and practice, being satisfied with the regulations of said church, may, upon organizing and adopting the rules and usages contained in our Book of Discipline, organize themselves into an Annual Conference, and assume and exercise their rights as such.

The Presidents of adjoining Conferences may make alterations in their boundaries respecting particular places and appointments, with the consent of the societies immediately concerned; all which shall be laid before their approaching Annual Conferences for adoption or rejection.

Section XXVIII.

Course of Study

For Probationers and Preachers in the Methodist Church.

FIRST YEAR.

The Bible—Doctrines.

The existence of God; the Attributes of God, namely—Spirituality, Eternity, Omnipotence, Ubiquity, Omniscience, Immutability, Wisdom, Truth, Justice, Mercy, Love, Goodness, Holiness; the Trinity in unity; the Deity of Christ—His Humanity—Union of both; Personality and Deity of the Holy Ghost; Depravity,

Atonement; Repentance; Justification by faith; Regeneration, Adoption, Witness of the Spirit, Growth in Grace, Christian Perfection; Possibility of Final Apostacy; Immortality of the Soul; Resurrection of the Body; General Judgment; Rewards and punishments.

[The examination on the above to be strictly Biblical, requiring the candidate to give the statement of the doctrine, and proofs.]

Systematic Divinity.

Watson's Institutes, Part First; Fletcher's Appeal; Watson's Institutes, Part Second; Shinn's Plan of Salvation; Clarke on the Eucharist,

The Bible—Sacraments.

The Sacrament of Baptism—its Nature, Design, Obligation, Subjects, and Mode. The Sacrament of the Lord's Supper—its nature, Design, and Obligation.

[Examination same as upon the Bible in the first year.]

[Read Wesley's Sermons and Notes;

Watts on the Mind; Whitehead's Life of Wesley; Watson's Apology; King and Stillingfleet on Apostolical Succession; and Snethen on Lay Representation.]

Church Government.

Constitution and Discipline of the Methodist Church.

[Read "Defense of the Truth," by McCaine.]

Composition.

Essay or Sermon.

Common English Studies.

English Grammar, Ancient and Modern Geography.

SECOND YEAR.

The Bible—History and Chronology.

Candidates to be prepared upon the leading events recorded in the Old and New

Testaments; Reference Books—Horne's Introduction.

Systematic Divinity.

Watson's Institutes, Parts Third and Fourth; Butler's Analogy.

[Read Smith's Hebrew People; Mosheim's Ecclesiastical History; Townley's Illustrations of Biblical Literature; Watson's Sermons; History of the United States.]

History, etc.

Outlines of History; Rhetoric; Logic; Moral Science. Text Books to be chosen by the respective Annual Conferences.

Composition.

Essay or Sermon.

[Read Rollin's Ancient History, Smith's Patriarchal Age, Historyof the Methodist Protestant Church, S. K. Jennings' Exposition, Prideaux's Connections.]

Section XXIX.

Forms.

Form of a Release from a Circuit or Station.

A—— B——, the bearer, is hereby released from any further obligation to continue his ministerial labors in —— circuit or —— station; and is also entitled to this testimony of his good moral standing in the Methodist Church.

C—— D——, President
——Annual Conference.

Form of a License to Exhort.

A—— B——, a member of the Methodist Church, residing in the —— station, is hereby authorized to exercise himself, on all proper occasions, in exhortation, and calling sinners to repentance.

This license to be renewed annually.

Signed by order,
And in behalf or the Qr. Con. of ——.

E—— F——, Chairman,

C—— D——, Secretary.

January 1, 1867.

Form of a License to Preach.

C—— D——, a member of the Methodist Church, residing in —— circuit, being duly examined by this Quarterly Conference, on gifts, grace, and acquirements, is hereby authorized to preach the gospel of Christ.

This License to be renewed annually.

Signed by order,
And in behalf of the Qr. Conf. of ——.

J—— K——, Chairman.

C—— H——, Secretary.

January 1. 1866.

Renewed January 1, 1867.

J—— K——, Chairman.

C—— H——, Secretary.

Form of Elder's Credentials.

To all whom it may concern, Greeting:

Be it known, That C—— D——, having been elected by the —— Annual Conference of Ministers and Delegates, was ordained for the office of Elder, in the Methodist Church; and he is hereby authorized by said Conference, so long as his life and doctrine accord with the Holy Scriptures, to administer the Lord's Supper; to Baptize; to celebrate Matrimony; and to feed the flock of God, taking the oversight thereof, not as a lord over God's heritage, but being an example to the flock.

Signed by order and in behalf of the P—— Annual Conference.

N—— S——, President.

A—— C——, Secretary.

January 1, 1867.

Form of Recognition Credentials.

To all whom it may concern:

This is to certify that —— —— has

been recognised and admitted by the —— —— as a Minister of the Methodist Church; he having been duly ordained according to the usages and Discipline of the —— —— Church, of which he has been a minister and member. And he is hereby authorized by said Conference, so long as his life and doctrine accord with the Holy Scriptures, to administer the Lord's Supper; to Baptize; to celebrate Matrimony; and to feed the flock of God, taking the oversight thereof, not as a lord over God's heritage, but being an example to the flock.

Signed by order, and in behalf of the aforenamed ———— Annual Conference.

B—— F——, President.

A—— G——, Secretary.

Form of a Certificate of Membership.

The bearer hereof, T—— W——, an acceptable member of the Methodist Church, being desirous of removing from this station, is entitled to receive, from the undersigned, this certificate of his good standing.

W—— G——, Superintendent.

B—— Station, January 1, 1867.

FORM OF A CERTIFICATE FOR AN UNSTATIONED MINISTER OR PREACHER, WHO DESIRES TO REMOVE TO ANOTHER CIRCUIT, STATION, OR DISTRICT.

The bearer, S—— B——, an unstationed minister of the Methodist Church, being desirous of removing from this circuit, is entitled to receive from the undersigned, this certificate of his good standing.

W—— P——, Superintendent.

F—— Circuit, January 1, 1867.

Form of a Certificate

FOR A STATIONED MINISTER OR PREACHER WHO DESIRES TO REMOVE TO ANOTHER DISTRICT.

The bearer, J—— L——, having fully complied with his engagements to the ——— Annual Conference, his moral character standing fair, and being desirous of removing to another District, is entitled to this certificate of his good standing.

A—— S——, President of the M—— Annual Conference.

January 1, 1867.

Form of a Transfer.

The bearer, A—— S——, of the O——— Annual Conference, having consented to be transferred to the M——— Annual Conference, is hereby duly transferred.

C—- S——, Pres. of the O—— An. Conf

E—— H——, Pres. of the M—— An. Conf.

January 1, 1867.

Form of Certificate of Election.

This is to certify that A—— B——, was. duly elected a delegate to the Annual Conference of the District, to sit in on the day of 18 by the of the

A—— R——, Chairman.

S—— P——, Secretary.

Forms of Certificates of Election.

A—— B—— was duly elected by the Electoral College of the M—— District, held on this day of 18 a ministerial representative to the General Conference of the Methodist Church, to sit in the city of on the day of 18

G—— H——, Chairman.

P—— S——, Secretary.

E—— F—— was duly elected by the Electoral College of the M—— District, held on this day of 18 a lay representative to the General Conference of the Methodist Church, to sit in city, on the day of 18

G—— H——, Chairman.

P—— S——, Secretary.

INDEX.

CONSTITUTION.

DISCIPLINE.

www.ingramcontent.com/pod-product-compliance
Lightning Source LLC
LaVergne TN
LVHW021417110826
845150LV00007B/1962